Suburban Locust

ANTOSH WOJCIK

BAD BETTY PRESS

First published in 2025 by Bad Betty Press
Cobden Place, Cobden Chambers, Nottingham NG1 2ED

badbettypress.com

PB ISBN: 978-1-913268-78-7
EPUB ISBN: 978-1-913268-79-4

A CIP record of this book is available from the British Library.

Cover artwork by Coco Eryss
Book design by Amy Acre

Printed and bound in the UK by TJ Books, Padstow, Cornwall
using FSC® Certified paper from responsibly managed forests

SUBURBAN LOCUST

Antosh Wojcik is a poet, drummer, community artist, sound designer and co-founder of Sleepwalker Studios, a Dorset-based production company. His drumming and spoken word theatre piece *How To Keep Time: A Drum Solo for Dementia*, produced by Penned in the Margins, toured internationally in 2019, supported by Arts Council England. He has composed and sound designed for scripted and documentary films such as *Alo* (selected for BFI's London Film Festival & Sundance London, 2023/24), *The Memory Boom* (competing at Tallinn Black Nights Film Festival, Rebels With A Cause category, 2024) and *Camel Before The Storm* (commissioned by Natural England & Arts and Culture, University of Exeter, 2025), all directed by Xenia Glen. *Suburban Locust* is his debut poetry collection. His work explores memory, heritage, labour, time and the destabilisation of these things.

CONTENTS

Suburban Locust

MAKE AN EXIT

Sis, let's call her M, comet of shout,
bags everything in her room,
napalms out, smokes the landing.
Dad, let's keep it Dad, drunk
on fiasco, curses her abandoning.
As she splits, M threatens to torch
his sacred lawn so he finally learns
the cost of his worry. My worry,
gregarious and nomadic as his,
drives me after her score across the suburb.
We're in the river, sis.
At the door of the crisis house,
M introduces me to her other family:
a swarm of sandy dudes with compound
eyes and small-talk-like clicks. These people
make her happy. I press the last
of the money into her hand,
knowing it will turn into tunnel hours.
I hug her, the smell of ash cloud absent
for a moment. On the walk home,
I sing in my first accent to get to Texas,
to the swingset we'd drop from,
training our bungee-muscle, the sun
grinding us down with its ancient thumb,
days so hot that falling
from the sky was all we could
do to cool down.

EQ'ING M'S EARTHQUAKE

– Modified Mercalli Intensity Scale, adapted
from the United States Geological Survey

0 – 30Hz.	Felt by equaliser and angels. Not heard.
30 – 60Hz.	Felt only by nerve, gut, parents, brother. Vibrational: door frames and floorboards uneased by bass frequency.
60 – 100Hz.	Felt by neighbours returning from nightshifts on upper floors of buildings. Standing cars rock. Passing of a truck. Many do not recognise it as earthquake.
100 – 300Hz.	Light sleepers awakened. Dishes, windows, doors disturbed. Walls may make cracking sounds.
300 – 600Hz.	Felt by nuclear families. Heavy sleepers awakened. Pendulum clocks stop. Dishes and windows break.
600 – 1kHz.	Many frightened. Family pictures are knocked off walls. Fallen plaster. Heavy furniture poltergeisted. Heavy truck striking building.

1k – 3kHz.	Difficulty standing. Considerable damage to poorly built structures: parents, patio, petunias.
3k – 5kHz.	Partial collapse. Particle collapse. Columns, monuments, walls topple. Steering is affected.
5k – 7.5kHz.	Structures thrown out of plumb. Gaps in tarmac, craggy veins. Substantial damage, parental collapse.
7.5k – 11kHz.	God's well-built wooden structures pulled from roots. Most masonry destroyed. Rails bend. Time bends. A great white coo occurs. Ravines in the suburban streets. Driveway disarray. M is nowhere to be seen.
11k – 14kHz.	Few, if any, remain standing. New neighbours appear. Locust swarms materialise. Thoughts struggle to materialise. At this point, I recognise the earthquake.
14k – 22kHz.	Total damage. Voids swallowing land and structure. Lines of sight and level distorted. Objects, felt yet unseen, thrown into the air. M is void. EQ no longer registers the earthquake.

SEER

There was an all-seeing bachelor
who captured the great earthquake
unfolding in high fidelity
on his CCTV cameras wired across
the suburb—a biblically-accurate
angel of surveillance. The stoner's prophecy
had come to pass, the teen
babbling about a cloud of teeth
swallowing the real estate.
If only he'd listened,
thought the seer, as his eyed
castle was eaten by the great
white maw of the opening earth.

CERAMIC

We gaze into the earthquake rupture,
the score of our neighbourhood.
The lip of the fracture has something
ceramic about it, a dodge of brittle
lightning. On it goes to distant lands.
Suburbanites clutch the walls of the landscape wound.
Neighbours, postie, bus driver, attorney.
I look to my associate.
'Will they try to heal the wound?'
My associate shrugs. They move to the edge,
peer in, note something on their clipboard.
'It's dinner time,' they say.
Bang on 7.30, I'm looking into the ornate fish-shaped dish
my Babcia brought to Britain in the post-war move—
'It's Ceramika Bolesławiec, honey'—
flecks of salmon, desperate remains, clinging on.
'I have no idea why I'm hanging on,' I say.
'She returns,' says my associate, nodding to the window.
As the earthquake makes its way to us,
they open the fridge, discard the chutneys
then shelves and gesture that we step inside.

LEWISVILLE, DALLAS, TEXAS

I long to know the peace
        of the air with so much
air inside it becomes
        thunder, Texan pressure.
Your lone starriness
        cratered our first suburb
named Lewisville.

Lewisville, where you landed.
        Named Lewis after all
the Lewises who put
        their names in the names
of the people there first.
        You will only find
Lewises after this.

After this, the half-trigger,
        half-boot shape of Texas
is scored earth to fill.
        And as you were born
of Dallas, you are from
        the meadow dwelling
and lightning fields.

I dare the lightning,
       take hold of its levers
cranking out the weather
       while God is on business.
I take on the responsibility
       without knowing the consequences,
without knowing the thunder.

Without knowing,
       the earthquake's following you,
a consequence
       of your design. If you find Lewisville, Dallas, Texas,
know it's by design.
       I wept the weather a hundred years.
I've seen what makes us.

BURY IT

The vision: tru-lawn astro-turf. Lewis #1,
the grass replacement man, scalpels away the turf
in beautiful squares of breathing, exposing soil
and Cousin Jack, who's somehow been sleeping
below since Easter, wearing the same white tee.
He blokily resumes the Easter conversation,
as if waking from stasis. The gents send him
away, resume the turfing—Lewis #1's certain
Dad won't see a cloud of teeth anytime soon. For good
measure, Dad buries the ambered locust he stole
from Texas with a prayer, for what follows
him is more than teeth and may not be so neatly
concealed below this rug of grass
twitching in the wind so true, so worried.

LOCUST

worry the least | worry the tax | worry the pension |
worry the electric | worry the time | worry atemporal
pests | worry the white flight | worry the children |
worry the design of a heart | worry the pre-planning
| worry the scaffold | worry the decision | worry the
commitment | worry what's predetermined | worry the
path through the woods you've taken | worry | worry
the career | worry the frontier | worry the expedition |
worry the yield | worry the gregarious and nomadic |
worry the plague | worry the convenience | worry the
idle | worry the black widow at a kid's party | worry
the hail | worry the job the job the job | worry the end
| worry how the start went | a brother's worry | amber
worry | worry the evidence | worry what eases | worry
the earthquake follows you |

ST. FAILURE

And so the father took the chainsaw
to his daughter's wardrobe,
hinged the doors to his shoulders.
The doors, now wings, would carry
him to her so he may convey The Word.
His disciples gathered,
prayed for his levitation. He jumped,
from her window, face-planted
the neighbour's drive, becoming
a doorway into the betraying earth.
Drawn by his gravity, the disciples
tried to enter his back,
but he could not let them in, for he
had mastered what is kept inside.

WHEN OUR FATHER
WAS A BLIMP

Our father took to helium
and tethered himself to the roof.
There, he trembled
like a first-day safety flag
until he covered the sky.
His meat was undeniable.
We used to throw javelins
for nervous behaviour,
but our weaponry
and ability to challenge
had been tamed as he reached
his final overblown state.
Man is man, even at this scale.
The blood sleet of our father
began to wilt the petunias.
New strains of fish in the pond;
angsty carp, bloodshot and hungover.
We boys prayed to him
about our sexual encounters;
still inflation evades us!
Our father knew only too well.

A TEEN CALLED AMBER

mum and dad warn you of the bad area
you only know a bad area once you know
and you end up there without planning
the urban bleed from suburb to chaos
a teen called Amber confesses their schizophrenia
as you navigate the labyrinthian estate
back to the party hosted by identical twins
young women you fancy too much to speak to
you and Amber dressed in lab coats
as if in examination of the orderly council
chaos maze you dressed as the same thing
Amber confesses they know the gang tagged
in graffiti along the walls and if they show
Amber will most likely punch anyone until
fizzing pulp including you for you could be
one of them for all they know and you don't
know if that's actually how this works or
if Amber is your imaginary friend returning
from the Texan suburb after all this time
and you should rejoice in the maw of chaos
for if they can escape you can too

THE WOOSE

no one thinks it was the first electrician
no one believes it was a flying woman
some say it was a gelatinous mud shark
some propose it was an orphaned wild man
no one knows it was a disaster
no one blames it for running away
some reckon it wears feather tights
some assume headlessness
no one depicts its slimy physicality
no one describes it as a feeling
some hypothesise it is the juice of the unripe plum
some realise it's history oozing
no one senses they may be talking around the thing
no one differentiates a beast from a man
some appreciate the ambiguous being
some acknowledge the gender disruption
no one claims to have married it
no one declares their love for it
some allege its fingerprints
some reexamine the evidence
no one knows what the Woose is
some say the Woose named the Hill
everyone lives on Woosehill
everyone is the Woose on the Hill

ROLLERCOASTER

Before the bunk bed was sawn in half
and lived out its days in existential dread
in separate rooms, I called top bunk
and lay above my brother, Steve.
Worry-waked and fearing death by
excessive swallowing of toothpaste,
the popcorn ceiling swarmed and Steve
ran his feet in the slats of my bunk,
playing the sounds of a rollercoaster
until the comforting swarm descended.

BARNEY

the brother   alarms
and ambulances in his blood
no action   idle as clay
idle as raised
laminates the suburb
drives the blood
through the   plastic roads
like his kid self did
he rigs the homes   to joy
to flush the M-Kat out
he seals   the score she set
the suburb   playset
drives his bloody toys
thick as a cop to dead ends
dark squares   never known
the brother   the desperate
dresses as Barney does the jolly
calls her name to remind her
of Texas   but there's no reverb
in a vacuum suburb no carry
to the voice   Barney can't work
the empty costume
the discarded purple dinosaur
thrown to the woodchipper
the suburb playset
thrown to the woodchipper
the woodchipper
thrown into itself

the woodchipper woodchipping
the woodchipper
did you have that playset?
kid self reset
reset the blood, kid

LAWNACHE

What the lawn conceals
is an ordinary mystery.

Mum wants the grass replaced
with something that won't breathe,

so employs the last man
who clipped my sister

to install nu-turf.
His hands know only damage—

he will scalp the lawn
and expose the soil beneath.

I've buried my harms and lusts
in the lawn. It aches.

The night before, I dig
up our previous animals,

their bones in shoeboxes,
the sparrow whose last hum

I squashed, and fossilised
pornography.

The worms have eaten
through the bodies.

Shame is best slaked by regular burials.
I pat the grass goodbye,

my bladed friend,
my first conspirator.

RECITAL

Dad's first recital on the bank of the Vistula river,
warming his lips with the slurs, wet judder of a propeller.

We're joined by a congregation wearing parachutes
from the last church standing.

From the snout of his trombone a single godly drone,
somewhere between A & A♭,

to commemorate Babcia's brother, Stasek,
a pilot that never returned.

Sure as the note, he rises from the rushing water, part plane,
the wreckage fused with his body.

The powder of bombed Warsaw gently falls, we with it.
Stasek, a brass angel, soars through the dissolve of it all.

What a note it is.

TOURIST

The hooded spirits came to tea
and drew a glyph on the mattress.
I soaked their curse in the bath.

Juiced-up, I visited a bleak gallery
and wept. Murals to flattened suburbs
stretched for kilometres.

One of the bombers was skinned,
turned into an inclusive disco hall.
A weapon can be reclaimed by dance.

The bloc erupted into flames
I only felt in my dreams.
Young Polish people live on

in a hated place. Like a curse,
I carried on
making marks.

SLICE A CITY

Serve a flattened city
by the half slice,
half of the streets
will come back to you.
Stand in the same spot too long,
pay ground rent on your shadow.
Brutality, a concept
I learnt at a health store
once I saw where the dates were from.
At least they were organic,
pitted, de-shelled individuals.
Be careful,
be careful, the name of an uncle,
a paratrooper shot down,
stuck in a cherry tree
no longer standing
pitted, only recalled in memory,
casual as coffee on a porch
lit with fleas.

PAST YARD

So came the drought.
Dad asked me to imitate
rain in the backyard.
This was big.
Impersonating a shower,
I held my hands
above the dry patches
of grass. I thought
about all the rain
I had in my head
from being English.
Years and years
of it arriving on days
unexpected, mostly expected
but when it wasn't wanted.
Soon, I got a dry mouth.
Parched, I went indoors.
Dad drained a lemon
into my mouth
then sent me back to the yard.
Rain came from my hands
but nothing landed on the grass.
I stayed there 'til dawn,
'til bored. Come morning,
the yard had died.
There was a vague sense of loss
amid the patio slabs.

Dad fell to his knees on the dead
grass, shouting 'why' at a shroud
of locusts from the past.
They didn't stop this time.

DRILL SITE

The parents placate the firstborn with
a triceratops. He drills the horns into the carpet.
M with her skin so new, see through—he
has never seen what is below, so, tries to drill.
The parents punish the firstborn, wash
his mouth out with soap. The excavation must
be carried out elsewhere. He lays in the road,
the storm drains gurgling. What is below
the gurgle? Cloud-buffalo walk along
the sky chewing holes, loosing storms.
Rain pours on all things tarmacked,
the rain so hard like drilling, so hard
he can smell the undoing of the road,
the Texan gods waking below.

IN EVERY NEIGHBOURHOOD
A CHOIR

In every neighbourhood a choir
sings from the curb,

all-faith ancestral songs to soothe
the men of the households.

Dad seals the front door with glue
and requests we leave via catflap.

Still, the songs slip through.
'It's gone to shit since the choirs moved in!'

Dad says. The choir reminds him
he is Polish—it's disturbing, too much feeling.

He cannot slouch from the noise
of his blood. He must listen each time

he takes out the bins; the morning commute,
now a guilt trip. He lobbies the council,

whips suburban dads into revolt.
Streetsweeper vortexes scrub away

at the curb where the choirs stand
swallowing their voices in swirling noise.

All is quiet again. Walking the one way
of this place, you sometimes catch a sliver

of song from the gap in a window
where a teenager practises for their exam,

a teacher mentors on a dusty piano, a forgotten
trumpet is picked up for the first time in a century.

KILLING FIELD

until I am called
in for dinner   I play

in the garden
my killing field

of invisible things
re-culling invisible

millions of already
erased people

waiting in the caul
of play

until I turn amber
        my calling

sealing the practice
memorialised

museumed   rarely
mentioned

BUBBA-DEATH

Boys trudge up the shore with haystacks
of weed strapped to their backs, their gills
receding post-swim. One of them knocks
on the window of my sister's car—
'Bubba-Death, good shit,' he says.
He cuts a fillet off the stack, exchanges
for a wad. He walks on by as M grinds up.
She sourced it from a good warehouse in Cali.
The high is supposed to be 'woozy'.
She's thinking of transitioning from recreational
to entrepreneurial—she's got a client base,
there's demand—it just needs to be the right
strain. 'Whatever the dream is,' I say.
I watch the shoal of entrepreneurs carry on
their migration until the car fills with smoke,
my imagination dies and all is Bubba.

YARN

Mum medicates with yarn
to the calm of beige-think.
'What do you think
of the colour?' she asks.
'It's beige,' I say.

At the hostel, my sister fails
to hang herself with a curtain
tie-back on a mate's dare.
'Cheap materials,' Mum says.
'They wouldn't hold her.'

Holyer, the head teacher,
refuses to medicate.
Rope pours from the tap
whenever he is thirsty.
Find him 30 days late,
chandeliered.

Rope falls from the eyes
of his mourners, old mates
spinning holy yarns,
hanging their ties in the tree
out the front of school.

BAD NEIGHBOUR

It was the day the flying woman knocked on our door
and asked me to help her with something,
interrupting Mum's story about the electrician
she'd found dead in a river once—
'They shouldn't swim after all they've touched' she said.
I had left the teabag in my mug.
My brother, Steve, his face all airbag, still coming down
from inflation. Cashews. There's always something
trying to take away the people you love,
though I can't guarantee every nut has an agenda.
The flying woman insisted her wand was broken.
A good neighbour, I went over to her house.
She kept pointing at spots on the ground I couldn't see
and walked around them. 'Tread carefully,' she said.
In the kitchen, she cut lettuce, calling it 'daylight'
for Rainbow, her tortoise. We spent some time
pushing manageable chunks of daylight into the hole
where Rainbow's head comes out. The flying woman
gave me her butterfly net to catch dead things
on my way home. 'Tread carefully,' she said.
Home was seventeen steps from her house. I filled the net
with leaves from the driveway. A cuckoo headbutted
the Earth and ticked out of life on our doorstep,
its head smashed in. Its wings opened and closed for a bit.
The sky was too late. I scooped it up when the wings stopped,
catching it. I knocked on my front door. I waited and waited.

THE LAST GOOD NEIGHBOUR

I rake the leaves of the last good neighbour,
his humble wreckage behind the bins.
Syringe, baggies, and gutting equipment.
A reconstruction site. Perhaps he crawled out here,
a skeleton to reassemble with chemistry.
I found places like this in the woods,
shirts over wigwams concealing glass lung
support units. I know what to disturb
and what to leave, but even here, the hollowing
can happen indoors, near someone you love,
in supposed sanctuary, at a time of 'clean'.
There are so many leaves to rake.

HOTBOX

Hotboxer: Cosmonaut of the Suburb!
Benches their weigh-points for deals,
the woods, their public piss limbo.
Hotboxers turn cars into hand-aquariums
with their pricey exhalations.
Stoners submerge in their Fiat Puntos
sinking below the surface of field and street,
find government-disappeared aeroplanes
and a shifty landowner's underground meat lab.

M interrupts deer with her morning hotbox.
Bored of the sink, she tries above-ground
observation. The deer watch her car
then vanish in wheat. They rat her out—
the cops show and interrogate her trespassing.
'I'm taking a picture of that tree,' she yells,
pointing at a tree that isn't there,
as the cops float miles away,
dots in space with important questions.

GREAT WHITE

I took a job advertising some new blood pill
and walked the one-way system of the suburb
dressed as a giant heart. People threw fast food
from their cars. BMXers used my foamy body
as a ramp, trying to get blood to pump out of me.
'It's just a costume,' I yelled
out of the left ventricle. They stuffed me
with peaches. *Who takes peaches to a BMX park?*
Passed out 'til night-time—super unhealthy—
then took a backroad home. All the mansion burglar alarms
twinkled like rigged stars that would never sound—
who can afford to burgle a mansion,
you need artillery, right? A behemoth was hanging out
on a rooftop, TPing the facade with its arrowed tail.
It had the head of a great white shark,
eyes as deep as the heart of a shadow.
It was gasping and gasping.
'Do you need blood pills?' I started my pitch.
It sank to my level, opened its maw, a tunnel of teeth.
Suburbanites had convened along the street
behind me and were making their way
to the maw, humming things.
They were glowing. They carried offerings.
Swathes of people shuffled into the throat
of this great white thing to be swallowed by their deity.
Lost my commission like that. It unleashed
a great white coo and all was slowed. So empty feeling.
Didn't get to my door 'til sun-up
even though it's only a fifteen-minute walk.

STING OPERATION

We've carved 'M's into the benches
of the woods to draw you out,
lil' bath salt fiend. My associate

recommends the bloodhounds
but cautions your blood
may be too crystalised to track.

I imagine you pocked with geodes,
body shining with cavities.
My associate meows and shakes

a bag of Epsom salts
like they're tempting a lost pet.
Your return is welcome, anytime.

It's come to this. I'm a traitor
—I sold you out, brought the feds
in on my brotherly sting.

The night after each search,
I signal a flashlight
so the glow may catch on you,

so you know I only set out
to find you—not interrogate
or collar or trap.

REVERB

/

Go tell the crooked woods your name.
Tell it to the trees:
violin necks of a malformed church.

/

Call your name in the church with the roof
cut out, no god above, Dad cut Him out.
Let a rain in.

/

Let a laminate street carry no whisper.
Neighbours out. The milk no shows.
My last ambulance disrupts no one.

/

Dad, the aeroplane man, the salaried
runaway, his body the centre
of turbulence, emptied of dreams.

/

An empty house for mum is a cause
for decoration. Play the voices of workmen
as they wallpaper over ruptured plaster.

/

The NOS hit reverbs the head, plaster
3 sec laughter, food grade, charger,
blur mates to frostbite at nightspots.

/

Spot habit balloons, say gateway,
say nangs, say nitro to the plasticated
earthquake. Call your name. Call it gently.

/

WHAT RAIN

Dream where the earthquake
follows the daughter.

It rains terrestrial animals—
drugged bison, cows, M-Kats.

Must be Texas. Looking for M
in a wheat field, cyanide blue.

We were always going to end up here.
'Let go, let go,' she says.

What rain falls in a place
with no word for falling?

THE LOCAL PIT

In the Texas years of the family album
there is a photo of us looking down

on a T-Rex footprint in a riverbed.
Parents drove us out to the edge of a canyon.

It's probably a boating lake now.
Back then, were we thinking *jump?*

I think *jump* at the edge of the local pit,
to fall until my body is a fossil of light.

A golden wreck of a boy boats out on you,
hangs up a knife in your head instead

of a phone. A pit could be a telephone
for all I know. I'm calling out to you.

Who's to say you and I are not the same,
driven to the edge of the same ancient problem.

THE CELESTIAL PRINCIPLES
OF TURF OUT!™

You, who are stuck in the sod of your worries. You, who yearn for celestial plains anew, for fresh ground to claim as your own. Grab your gramps' shovel and Turf Out!™ It's time to dig yourself out of the dead soil and turf out the bad men cutting sod for a living, sods the lot of them. Turf Out! your dependency on TV and adverts claiming to have your best interests at heart. Turf Out! the hidden coke addiction, the mountain's mindful snow. Turf Out! the hits, the bumps. Turf Out! the horses cribbing in your arteries, the backfiring Ketamine exhausts. Turf Out! the racist, coastline-faced, union-jack-vested, foghorn-mouthed version of your Dad. Turf Out! your brother's past friends' comments on your breasts. Turf Out! his misjudged advice, his lack of answers. Shit moves at the speed of a shovel, as gramps always said, so Turf Out!™

LEWIS #2

We are Frankenstein. We are good men
and we shall forge the ideal Lewis for
our sister. If the world will not do it,
and God's not getting involved, we will
invent the Lewis of our tolerances.
We will forge for her Lewis #2. We learned
the manoeuvres of bad men, the tool
that is the lie that gets into the brain.
We are Frankenstein's sons. Lewis #2
will provide shelter as did our father.

Lewis #2 will not stoke the wildness
she thrives, will not love bomb, nor gaslight,
nor coerce. Lewis #2 will be the Lewis
of all Lewises until all other Lewises
are erased, are absorbed until he is total
Lewis and no Lewisian hurt remains.

THE THERAPIST

who I thought was my friend, Sarah,
wanted me for a shape project.

'Circling,' she called it. We will spiral
and sprawl all that is going on with you.

In the local desert, she draws a circle
around me. Three men arrive, shootout style.

They aim therapy cannons at me,
guns with microphone ends.

Speak your truth, they chant,
this is a safe space. No judgments.

Vultures orbit above, waiting for me
to be chunks, ponder whether

they want to ingest this kind of crazy.
Sarah is writing her findings

in pseudo-hieroglyphics in the sand.
'Sarah,' I say, but she is deep in the diagnosis.

'Sarah!' I yell. A sandstorm is picking up.
'I would have just gone for coffee.'

BREEZE BLOCK

What a mother wants for her birthday
        is the nuclear family intact.

Daughter, the hollow nomad, brings
        a breeze block to dinner.

I've baked Makowiec poppy cake,
        heavy on morphine.

Steve is in denial that we said
        no gifts this year.

Dad's in Texas and hasn't called.

My associate picks at burnt veggies with
        a gardening fork and doles out

facts about earthquakes in suburbia.

No one knows what they're talking about, save
        my sister who lightens like the breeze.

WORRY DRAWINGS

When Steve was a kid, he filled a *Draw Yourself!* sketch pad
with worry drawings: one completed each day, handed to Mum;

each self-portrait shaded in with a waterline from foot to scalp
to indicate how much panic he woke up feeling that day.

He wrote a percentage level on the chest in marker for clarity.
Worry Drawing #34 75% is titled 'Bites'—termites swarmed

his face mid-sleep, biting his eyes. He went to school bruised,
face all airbag. Questions came for Mum. 'Termites' she explained.

Worry Drawing #212 95% is titled 'Drowning'—I asked Steve
to lay in the shape of the worry drawing and strangled him

pneumonia-blue. Mum asked me about his neck bruises.
'Termites,' I explained, preoccupied with the remaining 5%.

Nowadays, Dad, overcome with the worry of locusts,
buys an air rifle and takes up shooting. The worry drawings

are targets, pinned along the fence. A headshotted tapestry
of my brother treading water.

SKIING

A lack of wilderness in the house
guts the nerve of its men.
We decided to go for dessert together.
I'd seen him worried much of my life
but didn't think it would be so
pronounced when alone with me,
his eldest, in a foreign country
miles from anyone we knew.
'They'll think we're lovers,'
he said as we walked into a place.
Something sloped
in me. A ski resort in summer
is its own sort of ghost.
Skiers are preoccupied
with descent, obstacles, dodge,
the body's velocity,
shit like that. They would notice
the bump in the middle of my nose
that ties me to his DNA.
Perhaps this is a previous avalanche—
his failure to teach me golf,
trying to train my hips
to hold and relax, to have
the tension and wild
of a landslide. First man to hold my hips,
first man whose hips I'm from.

Dessert was quiet.
I forked through the cap of tiramisu,
he burled his shoulders
and looked so far away, a fallen
skier, whose outline is barely visible
on the slope of a mountain out of season.

CRISIS ACTOR

There's an increasing demand for crisis actors to be deployed to sites of moral panic.

*

Fighting retirement blues, Dad takes the job and plays victim of a lawn controversy.

He is interviewed about a neighbourhood Nazi who mowed a swastika into his front lawn. 'Don't they know I'm Polish?' he says, a fact he seldom brings up.

The story headline reads *Suburban Radicalisation*. National debate and protests ensue.

'This is how one gives back to one's professional community,' Dad mutters mid-Sudoku from his lounger.

*

Back in the day, Dad was photographed for an airport systems magazine. He is smiling after consummating a deal. One hand offers a thumbs up, the other clutches a certificate.

Dad's body parts became open-source assets for stock libraries. His tags: [English perseverance] [knowledge] [vitality at 50] etc. Dad's body performs beyond his working life.

*

A missile is fired at a village. The bodies are found days later but they are so damaged, no one can recognise or name them. It's reported in the paper just before the Sports pages.

'They don't treat their women right,' Dad says from the lounger whose ethnicity has not been denounced. He stares into the Sudoku grid.

*

Dad looks at the broken toilet flusher. 'I should know how to fix this,' he announces.

He never gets the role of 'plumber'.

*

There's panic in the neighbourhood as the cultural background of their furniture is debated.

Ottomans, chaise longues and futons are dragged to the tyre fire.

Performing at a protest, Dad's soundbite: 'What have they got against foreigners, now?!'

*

No one is sure of their ethnic origin anymore. The
registrars might have forged their birth certificates
anyway. The majority decision is to place themselves on
the tyre fire, favoured over self-questioning and reading
some history books.

A couple of us protest the burning. 'You know, I don't
really know who Dad is,' says my brother, who I'm
sure is actually my brother, as opposed to a crisis actor
appearing as my brother.

Dad is the first on the fire.

EATING TRENDS

Babcia didn't know hounds had souls
until she looked into the eyes of a dead Weimaraner.

In Warsaw, everyone's short-term memories
are pecked out of their heads by starlings.

You can buy freeze–dried bugs for grazing.
There's a coffee joint selling lavender hot choc

and bowls of jasmined locusts. We deserve it.
Satanists still buy Coca Cola.

I drank from the B'n'B waterbed and still,
Satan didn't show.

Time moves on, eating itself.
We hang on the air as the remains of its habit.

My currency is four of itself here.
Two weeks not worrying about the electric.

The storm's not letting up.
Pass the sauce would you.

PANNING FOR AMBER

From a crooked forest
        comes crooked sap.
Panning for what's golden,
        we hope to be,
and, fearing the swarm,
        we pan amber
from Gdańsk's shores.

We melt the fossil resin,
        mould it into a giant pill,
step inside,
        become inclusions
and continue
        our conversation.
In the future,
        the locusts will dig up
our words, our questions.

Once our golden pill
        is eaten through,
we will stand
        on the lulling shore.
My friend will ask me
        to take them to the crooked forest
so they may see the trees
        pretending to be music notes.

I will not take them there
        for my pretending will be done,
the air alive
        with the chattering wings,
with mandibles sharp
        from shearing the crooked pines
of their music.

DAD AT THE END OF THE WORLD

There wasn't much left, just Dad on an island, clutching his rifle.
The amber of Polish water washing up the shore
trying to pull him back to his blood.

I visited him, dressed in locusts.
As there was no world, there was not enough ammo in the world
to shoot them from me.

I'd finally become the grass of the yard
and what had eaten him all his life
was eating me.

'Was it worth it?' I asked.
He didn't look at me, only the beyond,
aiming at the amber clouds of could-be swarms coming for him.

YOLKS

A spray-paint death of a man in the middle of the road.
Traffic guided around his outline.

At night, I walk back to him,
curl into the stomach of the drawing.

A dead man's birthmark on the earth.
Everyone wanted you here for longer, I say.

Maybe it feels like a baby kick on the other side.
Maybe he's the lid of heaven.

Pushing my face into the cakey tarmac
I see all sorts of swallowed.

Whole cars with families inside,
songs still fat on the radio.

Dropped fruit and newspapers.
Hail, on pause.

God's barbecuing above the sunken landscape.
We're all trying to be reborn, He says, flipping a burger.

Way, way down, the man who died is still sinking.
The tarmac stretches like yolk.

At home, I fry eggs, the whites
pooling as the dead man's outline.

Egg shells are porous. They pick up all sorts of ideas,
God remarks, dressed as my brother.

He takes leftovers from the fridge and scuttles off.
The yolk settles in the stomach of the man.

Pan, non-stick like the road.
Everyone wanted you here for longer, I whisper to the egg.

ACID HOUSE

an additive syncopated pantoum
after Will Tyas

this house cast out
our sister
its patterned walls
and soft furniture
remedy anarchy

our sister's anarchy
the new hobby
cast out the remedy
cast out our house
cast an extinct timezone

the parents holiday
in extinct timezones
our anarchy
remedy for the suburb's
patterned soft hobby

our new hobby
our parents' soft extinct
cast out the suburb
our sister patterns
anarchy our remedy

YARD SALE

Yard sale's been going for years now.
Every customer differs—the English
politely seize your goods with contracts
and agreements, Americans practically
yank the turf from beneath your feet,
lil' local landgrab, yard gangs hit
the hoods, I swear, whole yards gone,
the live-in gardeners running out
yelling as if a stolen garden over here
is the same as a carpet bombed place
over there. Picture the scene.
A yard sale on napalmed ground.
Cheap pitches, believe me.
You own it if you bomb it, right?
Kids fleeing home, mostly mouth.
My ex holidayed at the massacre fields
30 years later, six foot, kinda Aryan.
She was surprised that the local people
didn't like Westerners too much.
She flew there on pocket money.
Carboot sale rent-a-genocide.
Gone for six months and came back
with a far-offness in her eyes
all suburbanites have, you know?
Anyway, my Aunt Cathy's walking stick
is $30 and I'll throw her ghost in for free.
It's all got to go. Not much time left.

COD

We descended from fish,
crawled up on land,
not all of us lived.

We walk to a suicide height,
above the cliff's erosion
and survey this dumb island,

this place built on other
shores' belly gold.
M's inner looter awakens,

eel-mouthed from the drugs,
she claims that she'd move
to Sierra Leone

if it wasn't too dangerous—
my sister has no expertise
in danger or Sierra Leone.

She's just good at finding it—
danger, that is, doubt
she could find Sierra Leone.

One day soon we'll be back
in the ocean with everyone
we drowned,

suffocation, our expertise.
As fish-people, we stay
in a house of dusty puppets,

set in colonial dioramas,
my sister and I, stoned to cod
gasping at the ceiling.

PARSNIP

somewhere
the suburb
has ended
my associate
has ended
their study
homemaking
a humble life
in the score
it remains
to this day
they taproot
themselves
into the mud
the slough
the wose
sprout a rosette
from their head
so they may eat
their skin
ambering
to origin
they offer
their body
as suburb
for worms
chewing
commuters

in the under
amber child
continuous

DETOX ON NEPTUNE

M and I rent a shack on Neptune.
It's a long drive. It's sparse,
the tourist attractions few,
nowhere is open yet, the place
a long, vague blue.
'Just what I need,' says M.

Neptune's main attraction
is the wind. 'Winds of 10,000
miles an hour,' boasts the sign.
We step into the wind
to be stripped down
to what we are made from.

'You look like bad wallpaper,' says M,
'Like, really bad granny
wallpaper or granny rugs
and wallpaper, or granny rugs
and sofas and wallpaper. Really bad.'

It's cool feeling each bone let go.

'Can't believe this doesn't hurt,' M says.
The wind pulls the Texas swing set
from her, the golden wrecks of boys,
weed—you've heard all this before.

The wind goes on until we are bored
dust. Inside the shack, we sit in silence.
M turns on the TV set, tries to find
reruns of familiar cartoons but satellite
isn't here yet. We are the first.

GREENLAND MEMOS

i. Development – Phase 1

Big Weed greenlit Project: Suburbia! Our communal sculpture park, [an exhibition of block-frozen stoners curated Henge-style about Greenland, accompanied by replica hotbox cars in permafrost] is in development!

Current obstacles are the natives – refugee penguins. It is hard to determine their intentions and incentives.

ii. Development – Phase 2

We invited the parents of the stoners to attend a private view, conducting an evaluation to bid for future funding & marketing budget.

Their feedback is summarised as follows:

* this is a good neighbourhood
* so white and pristine
* my dear little snowflake, shining in stasis!

Also, turns out, the penguins were just curious. They're now in safe confinement!

iii. Exhibition

We had a good few months of opening until global warming turned Greenland into a beach resort! So the land for our sculpture park is no longer viable. Head Office were unsure about audience engagement also…

Big Weed are reorienting the scope of the development, folding it into Project: California 2. Tech companies are buying up real estate quick!

We had some feedback from the defrosted stoners that I wanted to share with you all.

Comments summary:

* I knew what it was to be… a plant
* … to be observed, man…
* thrivin'

Of course, the weather had to ruin our exhibition. Outdoor work is always a challenge. Remember though: Art and Permanence never go hand in hand!

At least those sweet little stoners are back with their parents.

We are putting in a bid for the next exhibition site. Project Title: Future Zoo for the Past. Inspired by those lovely anarchist penguins. Please get your requests in sharp – we are running out of volunteers, space and indeed, time.

LOST AMERICANS

A day to exhaust all options.
Inhaling on the exhaust pipe

at intervals to hawk up
the last couple days' meals and laughs,

then driving endlessly, 180 down the freeway,
in a scrappy vessel to find

our ancestry, tarmacked.
The sub bass filters out when you up gear.

'Swear this was America!'
Suck something fat-blue out the exhaust.

coughing 'Did I take a wrong turn?'
Gas is running out.

A crooked forest of raw music notes
grows on the freeway banks.

We're in the river, sis.
You pull into the drive-thru.

We eat junk food until we are junk.
Junk what we think.

Dad calls anywhere we drive
we don't know 'Bagshot'.

All options exhausting.
This must be it.

YEAR OF THE CHAINSAW

Drive your chainsaw
through the cradle
of this addict to test
if her angel shows up
in a power cut, ashed
up, ghosted out, M
you are the last shoes
hanging on the wire
clinging on for the dial up,
I'm with you, I grocery-
shopped all the 2ams
to chance you, Dad's love
a punch out in the dark,
the last garden we knew
was aflame but the cherry
tree still sketches out
its seasons in drooping
eternity, ringing with teeth-
shaped injuries, the ghosted
out suburb doesn't recognise
angels with grass wings
the shape of Texas
but the state of your cradle
will always welcome
you back, we made it
through the year of the chainsaw,
Dad's birthday regret,

he's dulled the blade's teeth
to swaying, you, lighting up
at the end of the world
casual, no locust can lick you
for your swarm of ash
is our cradle and you strip
the world of its earthquakes.

THE WILDEST SHIT

For M

Can't fuck up the dreams if there were none
to start with. Our parents patterned the idleness,
the safety net, the acid house, thought the love
was all that was needed, peace the comfortable
assumption, but you were your own boulder
of riot through the world, the engineer
of your own abandon, held down your job
while piloting the fizzy cosmos, through it,
don't regret it, you have seen the wildest shit,
no take backs, witnessed people at their full
without judgement and left unscathed,
save a few zebra marks. You ask why the fuck
NASA send people into the big blue wilderness.
I see you as a simple astronaut whose earthing
would break most ground, who sees me through
the locusts and sees me full, not eaten.

NOTES

All names have been changed or given aliases to safeguard and protect their identity. Furthermore, subjects provided sensitivity reads of the collection prior to publication.

These poems are a result of inherited displacement and occupation experienced by my Polish ancestors during WWII. The poems in this collection have been finished and live on during the ongoing genocide waged by the State of Israel on the Palestinian people. The poems are offered towards Palestine, and towards American Indian and Indigenous Peoples and communities, namely Alabama-Coushatta, Caddo, Carrizo/Comecrudo, Coahuiltecan, Comanche, Kickapoo, Lipan Apache, Tonkawa and Ysleta Del Sur Pueblo, to all who have experienced genocide, and all occupied peoples of the world.

The poem 'Make An Exit' owes the phrase 'bungee-muscle' to an Andy Craven-Griffiths poem containing the phrase 'bungee-blood'.

The poem 'Lewisville, Dallas, Texas' references Natalie Diaz' poem 'Zoology', particularly the line 'My mother had been weeping one hundred years...' It also refers to Walt Whitman's *Leaves of Grass*.

The poem 'Killing Field' refers to Bob Hicok's poem 'Bottom of the ocean', which also empowered use of the symbol of amber throughout the collection, in tandem with the labour practice of amber panning on Polish shorelines.

The poem 'In every neighbourhood a choir' began as a response to a RAP PARTY prompt from Inua Ellams and Theresa Lola.

The poem 'Panning for Amber' references, in part, Robert Frost's 'Panning for Gold'.

The form of the poem 'Acid House' is inspired by a far more impressive syncopated specular by Will Tyas.

ACKNOWLEDGEMENTS

'It takes a village...' Well, it's taken a suburb.

Versions of poems collected here have been published and anthologised in *Abridged, Action, Spectacle, Anthropocene, bath magg, Dizziness of Freedom* (Bad Betty Press), *Home* (Colliding Lines), *PROTOTYPE #3* (prototype) and *The Lost Art of Staring into Fires* (Valley Press). Thank you to the editors and publishers for believing in the work and bringing it to the world.

The poem 'Skiing' is dedicated to Gboyega Odubanjo who edited the poem for *bath magg* and was the last poem I shared with him live at a gig on this earthly plain. You are missed, loved and your writing continues to move the world.

The poems 'What Rain', 'Drill Site' and 'Detox on Neptune' are dedicated to Leon Priestnall, who heard early versions of the poems collected here and offered encouragement for my overall subject. You are missed, loved and you are integral to what these poems became.

Thank you to Roundhouse Poetry Collective cohort 2013-14, Barbican Young Poets cohort 2013-14 and the Burn After Reading Collective for years of nurturing spaces to test and share work. I would not be here without you nor the producers who supported my development. To every poet and writer I've crossed paths with, shared a stage/space and whose work I've read, your artistry has shaped me and continues to do so —I'm forever grateful.

Thank you to my mentors, Bohdan Piasecki, Jacob Sam-La Rose and Kayo Chingonyi for showing me the path to these poems, for the opportunities, your encouragement and support over the years. Thank you for contributing words to the book and for being poetry heroes.

A further thank you to Hannah Silva for her kind words on the book—and for the work you make, for it gives so much permission to artists to use language in the most incisive, uncompromising ways.

Thanks to my University of Winchester lecturers Julian Stannard, Glenn Fosbraey, Vanessa Harbour, Calum Kerr and Brian Evans-Jones who showed me I was a writer and pushed me to find new planes of expression. You started this!

Thank you to Tom Chivers for reading the initial manuscript and encouraging me to get the book into the world—and for your championing of my voice over the years. A further thank you to Matt West for over a decade of encouragement, poetry fun and spiritual discussions leading to more and more joy.

Love to fwrdmtn★ - Darius, Jake, Tice, Myles, Hamish, Toby, Kareem.

Thank you to Coco for the locust artwork. I hope this is the start of many collaborations!

Thank you to Amy Acre and Jake Wild Hall at Bad Betty for your trust, your rigour, your belief and the light you bring to this writing. It's been a beautiful journey. I hope we do more.

A huge thank you to friends who have stuck by me—to Nick Murray, to Lamia Renaud, to Sam Morton, to Joel Auterson, to Paul Blatch, to Matt Elphick, to Adam Kammerling, to Dean Atta, to Amy George, to Yemi Adegbulu, to Owen Earwicker, to Ri Baroche, to Jane and Richard Evea. Your light and hearts keep this language alive.

Thank you to Venus and Paul for the company on writing breaks, the home-grown veg and beautiful surrounds in Dorset while I finished this work.

Thank you to my family, for understanding my pursuits as a poet, with this book and for encouraging its publication, for your love and compassion. Each poem is offered in love and remembrance of these challenges that we have made our way through. Remembering Babcia, Dziadek, Gramps and Nanny too. See you again down the river sometime.

Thank you to Xenia for your love, kindness and unfaltering belief in me. You made this book possible and I'm grateful, always.

M, these poems wouldn't exist without you, sis. Thank you for opening the world and showing me. Love you.